Stories about God... exploring faith perspectives in the primary classroom

Stories are a wonderful resource – engaging, sometimes surprising, often challenging. Well told, they can touch parts that other means fail to touch. If selected carefully and explored sensitively, faith stories provide important opportunities for personal and spiritual growth in the classroom.

Using story is one of the best ways of opening up questions and thinking about God with children. Too often there has been a tendency to concentrate upon the externals of religion and a reluctance to teach children about the central issues of religion. Talking about God with children is not nurture. Professor John Hull in his book *God-talk with Young Children* made the distinction clear. 'The emphasis should not be on teaching children the correct or orthodox doctrine about God. This clearly is a matter for religious communities. Rather the emphasis should be on enriching children's vocabulary, and through conversation, developing images and concepts which will enable children to grapple, at their own level, with the issues and experiences involved in God-talk'.

This book aims to provide story resources and some practical strategies to help teachers engage children in what Professor Hull describes as 'God-talk'. We have selected stories from five world religions which exemplify and make accessible some key teachings about God. The aim is to help pupils (and teachers) have fun and get talking, questioning and reflecting whilst getting to grips with some of the deeper messages and meanings the stories convey for believers.

Joyce Mackley
Editor

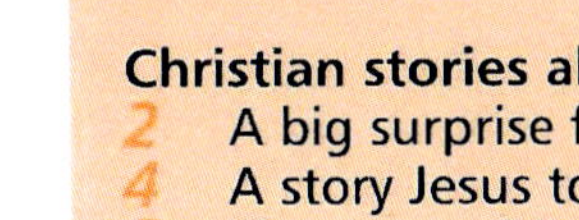

Contents

Three Christian stories about God

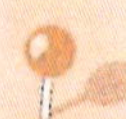

For the teacher

The following three stories are important in the Christian tradition. They connect to the three main ways in which Christians think of God – God the Father, Son and Holy Spirit.

The Annunciation is the story of when Mary finds out that she is to give birth to Jesus, the Son of God.

The story of the Lost Son is a story Jesus told about God the Father.

Pentecost is the story of the coming of the Holy Spirit who is God's guiding presence.

Each story has been rewritten to be accessible for pupils.

Fact file: Christian beliefs about God

- Christians believe in one God who created the universe and all life.
- They believe that God has become known to humans through Jesus Christ, the Son, who came to earth as a man and died for the sake of all humanity, and through the Holy Spirit who helps and guides people and is always with those who trust in him.
- God reveals himself in these 'three persons': God the Father, God the Son, God the Holy Spirit. This is known as the Trinity.

A big surprise for Mary!

One day Mary, a young girl about to marry a man called
Joseph, was at home in a place called Nazareth, when she
had a very surprising visitor. An angel! The angel said to Mary,
'Hello, Mary. God has chosen you and wants to do something very
special for you.'
Mary, was surprised and worried. What was going on?
The angel said,
'There's no need to be afraid. God is pleased with you. You are going
to have a baby boy, and you will name him Jesus.'
The angel sang a song about how great Jesus would be.
'I don't understand', said Mary. 'I haven't got a husband yet -
how can this happen?'
'God's Spirit will visit you', replied the angel. The baby is going to be
God's child too. Will you have this baby?'
Mary thought about Joseph. What would he say? She thought about
what God was asking her to do.
'If it really is God's plan for me … then I must do it,' she thought to herself.
'All right,' said Mary. 'I will have this baby for God.'
Then she went to stay with her cousin Elizabeth, who the angel said was
also having a special baby. When she arrived at Elizabeth's house, Mary
was so happy she sang a song to praise God. She felt so lucky to have
been chosen by a God who had the power to change people's lives.

(Based on Luke 1:26-56)

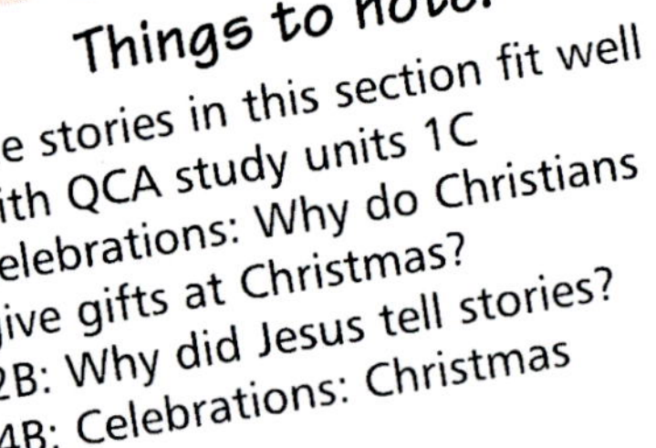

Angels are God's messengers
This message presents Mary with a choice about how she will respond to this big change in her life. Her experience of God changes her life. She accepts the angel's message even though this will be a challenge for her.

Things to note:
The stories in this section fit well with QCA study units 1C Celebrations: Why do Christians give gifts at Christmas?
2B: Why did Jesus tell stories?
4B: Celebrations: Christmas Journeys

An activity for younger pupils

Let's talk! Some questions to ask and respond to...

In the story Mary faced a hard choice...

- What was she asked to do?
- Who asked her?
- What questions might Mary want to ask?
- Have you ever been asked to do something really difficult – something you did not really want to do?
- How did you feel? (Pick out words from the **Feelings Box**.)
- What did you do?
- What helped you to decide?
- How do you think Mary felt when the angel came? (Use the words in the box.)
- Use these words to retell the story.

Activities for older pupils

1. **Exploring artists' impressions of the story**
- Look at some pictures of the Annunciation e.g. 'The Angel and the Annunciation' by Simone Martini, 'Annunciation' by Jan van Eyck, by Masolino, by Fra Filippo, all to be found in Sister Wendy Beckett's *The Story of Painting*. (Dorling Kindersley, ISBN: 0751311898)
How does Mary look to be reacting to her experience? How many of these reactions do pupils recognise from their own time of change?

2. **Talk!** In the Bible, angels are God's messengers. Pupils could (in pairs) talk about the angels in the pictures. What do the angels look like? What words might be used to describe them? What questions do pupils want to ask about them? Share these and suggest some answers different people may give.

3. **Angels** – exploring ideas using art:
   - Look at other images of angels (sculpture and other media). e.g. Anthony Gormley's Angel of the North; the opening scene of the film 'City of Angels', starring Meg Ryan and Nicholas Cage (powerful guardian angels protect the inhabitants of New York) or the classic film 'It's a Wonderful Life' (a friendly and caring angel).
   - If pupils had their own 'guardian' angel to help them at times of need, what might this angel be like?
   - Provide art materials: pupils could make a collage of their angel, using different shapes, colour, textures, words. Follow with creative writing: Imagine your guardian angel is watching over you. Write a story about how this might help you to face up to a difficult or challenging situation.

The Angel of the North, on a hillside near the A1 at Gateshead. By artist Anthony Gormley, it is made of steel and shaped like a jumbo jet and is Britain's biggest sculpture. It stands strong and powerful on the site of a disused coal mine. It symbolises hope and strength and the region's regeneration.

A story Jesus told about God: The Lost Son

Once there was a man who had two sons. The younger son said one day, 'Dad – I can't wait until you die before I inherit your money. Let me have it now!'

The father agreed and divided his money between his two sons. The younger son left home with his share, travelled far away and spent all his money on having a good time.

Then there was a terrible famine and people started to starve. The younger son had to get a job if he wanted to eat. The only one he could get was feeding pigs. He was still so hungry that he was tempted to eat the pigswill: yuk!

He was desperate. So he hatched a plan. He would go back to his father and ask his dad for a job. After all, his father's servants were well fed. He would ask his father to treat him like a servant. He knew he didn't deserve to be treated like a son any more – not after all he had done.

He set out. Before he had reached home his father saw him coming and was overjoyed to see his son again. He rushed out to meet him and hugged him. He didn't listen to his son's prepared speech, he organised a feast and a new set of clothes. The celebrations began.

The older son was angry and jealous. He had stayed at home and worked hard – he had never been given a party – yet here was his good-for-nothing brother – turning up again and being treated like a lord. His father, seeing this, went out to talk to him.

'Come and join in the celebrations', he said. 'You have always been a good son. But your brother has been lost from us ... but now he's back. He was dead and is now alive – let's celebrate his return.'

(Based on Luke 15:11-32)

**'Return of the Prodigal Son' by Rembrandt
www.gallery.euroweb.hu (use search engine)**

Drama activity for younger pupils

- Tell the story.
- Talk together about the main characters' actions and feelings. (Use the feelings box to support language – see page 3.)
- Work out and practise some gestures to show feelings such as sadness (the son in a far-off land); joy (the father on the return of his son); jealousy (the older brother).
- Act out the story in groups of 3 or 4.
- Decide together which is the most important scene in the story.
- Think carefully about where each character will be when they freeze, the expressions on their faces, their gestures and so on.
- Ask children to act out the scene in groups and freeze like 'living statues' at that point. Look together at one or two groups in 'freeze frame'.
- Talk about the message of the story at that point.
- Talk about the kind of person the father is – kind, forgiving, generous – and say that Jesus told this story to teach people that God is like this loving father.

This activity links well with the English primary strategy Speaking, Listening, Learning activities – Year 1 Term 3.

Activity for older pupils

Exploring a painting:
Painting: 'The return of the Prodigal Son' by Rembrandt
Website: www.gallery.euroweb.hu. Use the search engine to locate a full screen image of this painting. Display this picture on a whiteboard. After reading the story of the Lost Son ask pupils to:

- Analyse which part of the story the artist has chosen to show.
- Describe what is happening at this point in the story.
- Say why they think the artist chose to show this particular part of the story.
- Talk about how Rembrandt uses light and colour to show who is most important in the scene.
- Write a short paragraph explaining the message of the painting.

See also:

'The forgiving father' painting by Frank Wesley (*Picturing Jesus* pack B,) RE Today Services, ISBN 1-904024-44-0 16 visual images and classroom activities.

For the teacher

- Rembrandt's scene expresses the heart of the story as one of forgiveness, repentance, reconciliation and a father's love for his son.
- Christians believe God is like this father: he loves unconditionally and generously, no matter what people do wrong. His love never runs out.
- Richard Holloway, former Bishop of Edinburgh, emphasises how significant the father's actions would have been in that time and culture:

'We are told that the father, seeing him at a distance, ran to meet him ... the father's action was an abandonment of patriarchal dignity ... it was this action, this act of self-emptying, that finally changed the attitude of the son. His prepared speech ... now became a genuine act of repentance. The heart of the message of Jesus [is that] we become able to love when we know we are first loved ... this unconditional love burns through ... and changes hearts.'

The story of Pentecost - the coming of God's Spirit

It was now fifty days since Jesus had been crucified. His followers were trying to sort out all the extraordinary events that had happened since then. They were convinced that Jesus was not dead – that he had risen again. After all they had seen him, even touched him. They believed that he was the Messiah – the Son of God. But what were they supposed to do about it? They felt alone and a bit frightened.

Then, as they were gathered together on the day of Pentecost (the fiftieth day), it suddenly happened. Everything changed!!

What happened? Well, it was so strange they didn't really know how to explain it to people. They could only say that it was as if God's Spirit swept through the house, like a mighty rushing wind. It was as if each one of them had been touched by God's power – like a flame in their hearts. Whatever it was, they knew they didn't feel frightened or alone any more – they felt fired up, excited, full of courage!

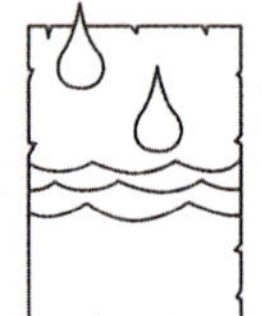

They rushed out onto the streets and began to talk to all the visitors in the city, telling them in their own languages about God's great work. People thought they were drunk until Peter explained, 'God's Spirit is pouring into us. This is a time when people will see visions and dream dreams because God is here!' Then he told all the people about Jesus – he wasn't frightened any more, he was brave enough to tell all those strangers the good news. Many accepted what he said and became Christians by being baptised. The Christian church had begun!

(Based on Acts 2:1-13)

For the teacher

- Fire, light and wind are Christian symbols of God's cleansing and moving power. Activity 1 explores these with pupils.
- Many believers find their strength in God and believe this is the power of the Holy Spirit working in and through them.
- Activity 2 uses an Ignatian style meditation to enable personal reflection. Saint Ignatius taught that God gives people strength and energy each day and that they should examine this.

Activity 2: Meditation on a candle

- Provide a candle/tea light for each pupil or table of pupils. Place inside a sand box to ensure safety.
- Use a stilling process to establish an atmosphere of reflective calm. This usually involves relaxation and attentive listening followed by focusing on an object or taking part in a visualisation activity.
- Read the meditation slowly, pausing after each sentence to allow pupils to reflect.

Meditation on a candle

Call to mind something which makes you feel strong and confident – it might be a person, a place, a thought. Hold it in your mind as you watch the candlelight.
What gives me energy and strength?
What has given me energy today?
What has drained my energy today?
What has given me courage today?
What has made me feel anxious?
What makes me feel fired up?
What dampens me down? Are there things I would like this flame to burn away?
Are there places I would like to take this light to let it shine? How do I feel, watching the candlelight?

Follow-up: creative writing activity

- Pupils could write a poem or piece of prose entitled 'Watching the Candlelight'.
- Support writing by writing the sentences from the meditation on the board as a prompt.
- Use candle-shaped templates for the final work. Create a Pentecost display.
- After writing their poems pupils could look at some Psalms which express how believers find their strength in God, for example Psalms 18, 23, 27 and 46.

Activity 1: Exploring the Christian symbols of fire and wind

- In groups pupils brainstorm or mind-map fire or wind.
- Record vocabulary in a web form.
- Each group agrees ideas and compares findings – identifying similarities and differences between groups.
- Pupils produce their own poems or creative writing expressing the symbolism of fire or wind, using the vocabulary.
- One simple structure for the poem is a cinquaine – a five line poem as follows:
  - 1 word – main subject
  - 2 adjectives to describe it
  - 3 verbs telling what it does
  - 4 words describing our feelings
  - 1 word – main subject.

Pupils produce a best copy and illustrate it with appropriate symbols and colours.

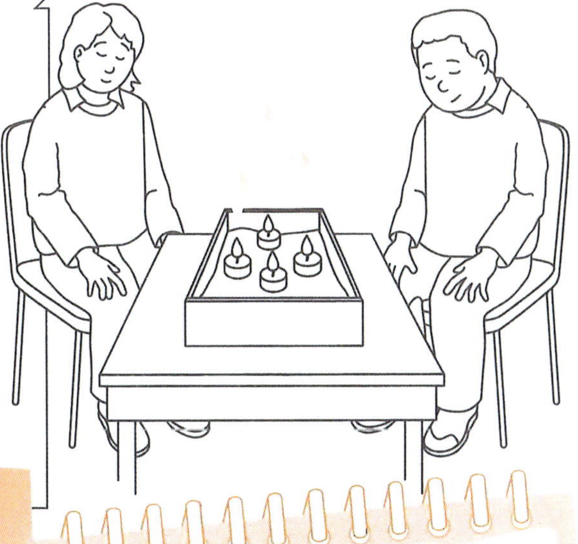

See also...

Stilling: For more details see *A to Z: Practical Teaching Strategies* by Mackley and Draycott (RE Today Services) ISBN1-904024-55-6

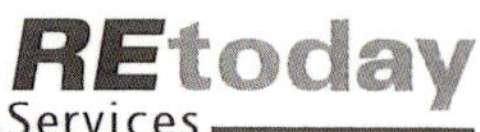

God the creator: a story shared by Jews and Christians

For the teacher

- The following story is found in the Jewish Torah and the Christian Bible.
- It is a simplified version for younger pupils, but the text is faithful to the biblical narrative of Genesis chapter 1.
- It introduces the concept of God creating the world and making it good in easy-to-understand terms.

In the beginning

DAY 1

In the beginning there was nothing except God.
Everything was dark.
God said, 'Let there be light'
And instantly there was light.
God called the light day and he called the dark night.
And he saw that it was good.

DAY 2

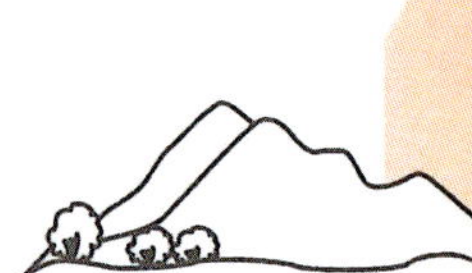

On the second day God separated the waters from the great space
And made a beautiful blue sky.
And he saw that it was good.

DAY 3

On the third day God made land appear from the waters.
He made oceans, seas, rivers and lakes. He made tall mountains, hot deserts.
He made trees, grass and flowers of every colour.
And he saw that it was beautiful and good.

DAY 4

God made two great lights. One for the day and one for the night.
He called the one for the day the Sun, and the one for the night the Moon.
God made all the stars in the universe.
And he saw that it was good.
The evening and the morning – a fourth day.

DAY 5

On the fifth day God filled the waters with fish and he made birds to fly through the skies.
And he saw that it was good.

DAY 6

On the sixth day God made animals of all kinds and he made people.
God was very pleased with what he had made. He saw that it was all very good.

DAY 7

By now God was very tired after all his hard work. So he rested!

Activities for exploring the Biblical creation story with younger pupils

- **Dance/mime:** Using the poem 'In the beginning' by Steve Turner on page 11, or similar, work out movements the children can use to show each stage of creation. Put these together as the poem is read.

- **Art work:** In groups pupils could paint pictures for each 'day'. Re-read the story to work out together what happened on each 'day'. Group 1: light; Group 2: sky/water; Group 3: land & plants; Group 4: sun, moon and stars in sky; Group 5: animals; Group 6: humans. Display paintings – count how many days – talk about what happened on the seventh day of creation and make the link with seven days of the week and how Jews keep Shabbat (Sabbath) special because it was the day on which God rested.

- **Talk about** the creation story: What does the story tell us about God? What words might describe him? Add these words to a creation pictures display.

See also...
Picturing creation, edited by Rachel Barker and Pamela Draycott, with original artwork by Kate Neale (RE Today Services, 2005, ISBN 1-904024-58-0): contains lots of ideas for exploring the creation story, seven full-colour A4 posters, and a CD ROM.

- **Creating:** Pupils create something using Lego/jigsaw or similar. How do they feel when they have finished making something? How do they feel when they break up what they have made? Link this to the creation story which teaches that God made something good – and how we are destroying it. How might this make God feel?

- **Drama:** Watch a clip of 'The Snowman' by Raymond Briggs or read the story of how James stands back and admires the snowman he has made. Children could be encouraged to ask and answer questions about how God might have felt when he saw everything he had made.

- **Look at natural objects** in detail – notice how stones/leaves are beautifully made and all different. Is this what we are like? Talk about how each of us is special and different.

- **Discussion and creative writing:** If children could create their own world – what would be available? What would they create? How would they create? Compose a class poem in which everyone contributes 2 lines using the starter: 'If I made the world it would be…' Extension: Perhaps older or more able pupils might talk about what they think about scientists being able to create a person – would it be a Frankenstein's monster? Is it right to try and do this?

See also:
'In the beginning' by Steve Turner in *The day I fell down the toilet* (Lion, ISBN 0-7459 3640-7) Song version available on 'Songs for the new millennium' (Breaking the chains, National Society and Methodist Publishing House)

The Lion Story Teller Bible by Bob Hartman (Lion, ISBN 0-7459-3607-5) - lovely version of the creation story for young children

Website containing animated creation stories suitable for pupils:
www.kids4truth.com/ eng_creation.htm &
www.just4kidsmagazine.com/ grandmaandme/beginning.html

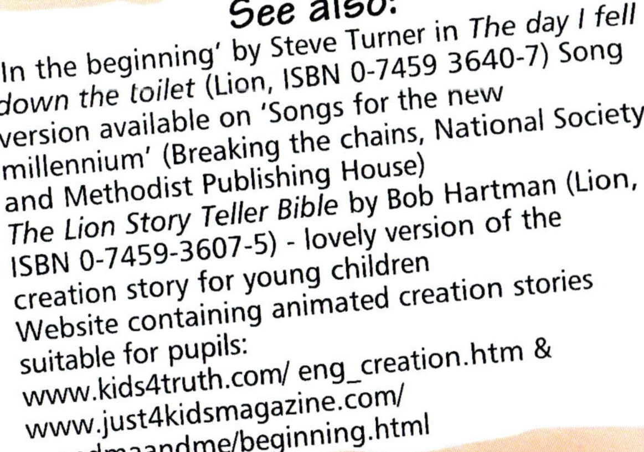

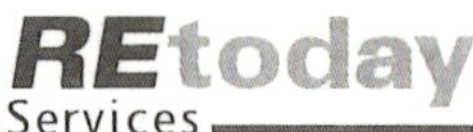

Helping younger pupils think about God the creator

1. Natural object

The following activity gives pupils the opportunity to focus and reflect on creation. Collect and explore objects from the natural world – flowers, leaves, stones. Make a display of these on a circular cloth. Pupils sit in a circle around it. Ask pupils to pick one item up and look at it carefully. **Talk about:**

- Do you think you could make that?
- Do you think anyone could make it?
- Where did it come from? Who made it?
- What does the creation story in the Bible say about this? (That God made everything and made it good.)

2. Psalm 8

Read the child's version of Psalm 8 (page 11). Ask children the following:
Can you tell me

- What do you think King David is looking at when he thinks about God?
- One thing King David asks God in this special song?
- A question you woul like to ask to ask God if you could?
- What do you think God is like if he can make these amazing things?

Introduce Christian and Jewish beliefs that we are all responsible for looking after these lovely things. Talk about how we can do that.

3. Follow-up activities

Pupils draw a picture of their natural object and complete the following:
If I had made this I would feel...............
I think that God/the creator must be...........................
I can help to look after the world around me by.................

Make a wall display or creation mobile of children's work and pictures of the natural world related to each day of creation, under a heading such as 'Jews and Christians believe God created the world'. The story is found in the Christian Bible and the Jewish Torah.

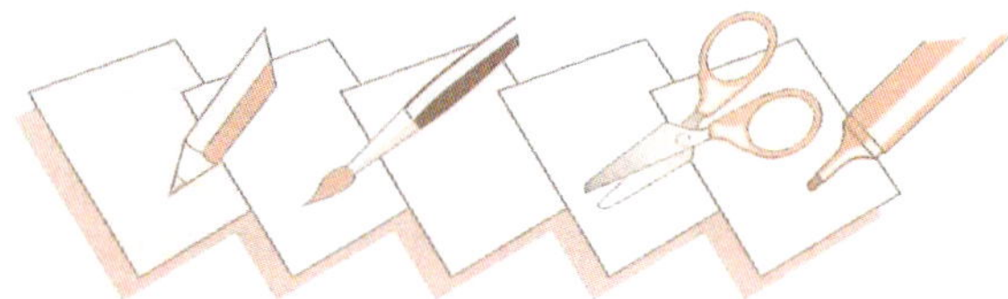

4. Circle activity

The following activity can be used to build on the idea that God made each person special.

Ask each child to name one person who is special to them and say why.

Second time round: Give each child the name of another in the group, ideally someone they are friends with, and ask them to say one special thing about that person.

Sophie is special because.........

Make a display of all the children's names and why each is special.
Pupils complete the following and add it to the display.

For Christians and Jews God is special because..........

For the teacher

Two different writers tell us about God the creator.

Psalm 8, a song of praise from King David written over 3000 years ago and recorded in the Bible.

A modern interpretation by the poet Steve Turner brings the creation story alive for younger children.

King David tells us about…

GOD THE CREATOR

Lord, our Lord, your name is the most special in all the world!

You are more wonderful than everything in the world, and your glory can be seen in the heavens above.

Children sing praises to you and say how special you are.

When I look at the sky you made with your fingers, I see the moon and stars which you put in place, and I wonder why you care so much about people when we are so ordinary?

But you, God, made people just a little bit lower than yourself … you made us special.

You, God, put us in charge of everything you made in the world.

You made us rulers over sheep, cows, wild animals, birds, fish and all the things that live in the sea.

Lord, our Lord, your name is the greatest in the whole world.

Psalm 8 – adapted for younger pupils

In the beginning

God said WORLD
and the world spun round,

God said LIGHT
and the light beamed down,

God said LAND
and the sea rolled back,

God said NIGHT
and the sky went black.

God said LEAF
and the shoot pushed through,

God said FIN
and the first fish grew,

God said BEAK
and the big bird soared,

God said FUR
and the jungle roared.

God said SKIN
and the man breathed air,

God said BONE
and the girl stood there,

God said GOOD
and the world was great,

God said REST
and they all slept late.

Steve Turner

From *The day I fell down the toilet* © 1996 Steve Turner, used by permission of Lion Hudson plc (ISBN 0-7459-3640-7)
Song version available on 'Songs for the new millennium' (Breaking the chains, National Society and Methodist Publishing House)

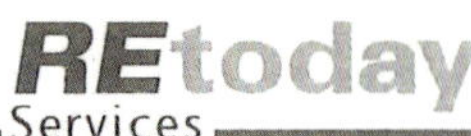

Jewish stories about G-d:

The story of Noah

For the teacher

- The story of Noah is sacred for Jews, Christians and Muslims. Avoid reducing it inappropriately to fit with classroom themes such as animals, transport or water!
- Good RE ensures pupils have a real understanding of the story's deeper meaning. For younger pupils this could be done through exploring themes such as danger, safety, obedience, promise, hope, G-d's action and judgement.
- The story of Noah is about the relationship between G-d and humans. G-d acts as a judge, finding people at fault for living selfishly. They are punished. Only Noah is saved because of his faith and obedience to G-d. The covenant, symbolised by the rainbow, is G-d's promise that never again will such 'punishment' be used.

Fact file: Jewish beliefs about G-d

Jews believe in one all-powerful creator G-d.

- Jews believe that G-d made agreements with their ancestors, Noah and Abraham. 'You will be my people,' said G-d, 'and I will be your G-d.' This promise is known as the covenant.
- G-d promised to protect his people and gave them laws to follow. The most famous ones are the Ten Commandments.

A retelling of the story of Noah for younger pupils

It is a time long, long ago, in a very hot country. You can hear a knocking sound. Knock, knock, knock! It is Grandad Noah - he is building a big boat. Get up from where you are lying under the tree and ask him if you can help. Grandad Noah explains that G-d has told him to build the boat, and he always does what G-d tells him to do.

It is a few weeks later now. Grandad Noah's big boat is finished. He has called it the Ark. Everyone in Noah's family has been busy gathering animals. Now is the time for them to go on to the Ark. What animals can you see? Can you hear them? Perhaps you can smell them?
What are you wondering? Have you a question you would like to ask? Think about it now.

It's getting very dark. Clouds are gathering. Noah is telling all his family to hurry up and get inside the Ark – that includes you! Suddenly you feel a drop of water on your neck. It has started to rain. Everyone hurries inside with the animals. The rain is getting heavier and heavier. Can you hear it on the roof? Can you see it from the windows? It is raining so much that the land is covered with the water. The water is rising. You feel something move … the Ark has started to float!

It has been raining for days and days now. You are fed up with all the rain and the noisy, smelly animals. Listen. You can't hear the rain on the roof any more. Look out of the window. It has stopped raining but all you can see is water – all around the Ark.

Grandad Noah has sent a dove to fly over the water to find dry land. You wait, wondering if it will ever return. After a while, the dove comes back. It has a twig in its beak! What do you think this means? Grandad Noah is very excited. Suddenly there's a bump, everything shudders. The Ark has touched land. Everyone is very excited.

Slowly the water is going down. What can you see? How are you feeling now? Grandad Noah is looking up at the sky and you look up too. You see a beautiful rainbow full of colour. Now you remember what Grandad Noah had said before the flood. He told you that G-d had made a special promise. G-d would send a beautiful rainbow as a sign of that promise. Grandad Noah is very happy. And so are you.

(Based on the Bible: Genesis chapters 6–9)

Things to note:

Many Jews do not write the name G-d in full out of respect for the commandment about not taking G-d's name in vain.

Activities for lower primary pupils

- Use a children's Bible to tell the story of Noah.
- Invite pupils to imagine they are Noah's grandchild. Use the 'guided visualisation script' on page 12 to retell the story. Pause often to allow children space to think and imagine. Follow this up with one of the activities below.

An activity for 5–6-year-old pupils
Drawing the pictures

- Ask pupils to choose two moments from the story and draw them both. One could be about 'danger' and the other about 'safety', or one about 'fear' and the other about 'hope'. Talk about how a picture can be moody: what colours for fear, and what for safety? Giving a picture frame and a sentence stem may help some pupils here.
- Pupils working at level 1 should be able to show in their pictures some of the outline of the Noah story (AT1) and be able to talk about ideas from the story such as fear and hope, danger and safety (AT2).

An activity for 6–8-year-old pupils
Raindrops and rainbows

- Ask each pupil to draw a large outline of a raindrop. Talk together about the story of Noah and identify things in the story which frightened Noah (for example: the floods rising) and how he might have overcome this fear (for example: talking to God). Ask pupils to think about a time they have been frightened and how they dealt with it. Pupils choose a fear or danger (either their own or Noah's) and write it on the raindrop. Illustrate it with pictures or symbols. Next choose some of these words: *safety, saved, escape, care, compassion, hope, destruction, promise, rescue.* Talk about how these fit with the story. On a large piece of paper draw a rainbow. Using some of these words write four lines (a poem?) into one of the rainbow colours. Mount all this as a class display.
- Pupils working at level 3 should be able to identify some key ideas in the Noah story and be able to compare some of their own experiences with these.

An activity for upper primary pupils
Noah's prayers

- Ask pupils to choose one of the following 5 moments from the story:
  - when God tells Noah about the flood because the people had been bad
  - when the animals are being awkward, and won't go in
  - when the flood floats the ark
  - when the dove flies away (or back)
  - when the rainbow appears, the sign of God's promise.

For the moment they choose, pupils write the prayer that Noah said.

This activity can done in pairs, drafting and redrafting for the best outcome.

Pupils working at level 4 will be able to show understanding of how religious feelings can be expressed and be able to handle questions and answers about a religious story (AT2).

For further reflection

Talk about how God hoped for a future in which people would lead better lives. What might make God angry about today's world? What is needed to solve these problems?

Jewish stories about G-d

The story of Moses and the burning bush

Key themes:
God's care for his people
God's power
The obedience and faith
of Moses

Moses was a shepherd and spent most of his time wandering alone in the land of Midian looking after his sheep. One very hot day, he noticed something very unusual. It looked like a bush that was on fire but it wasn't being destroyed. He went closer to investigate, but jumped back in shock when a voice spoke to him.

'Take off your shoes, and don't come any closer', ordered the voice. 'This ground is holy!'
'Who are you?' asked Moses, trembling with fear and looking around to see if someone was playing a joke on him.
'I am G-d', said the voice. Moses kicked off his shoes and hid his face. Now he really was afraid. 'What do you want with me?' he asked.
'I have been listening to my people, the Israelites, living in Egypt, replied G-d.
'I'm an Israelite. I used to live in Egypt', said Moses.
'I know', said G-d. 'Now listen to me.' Moses stood still and listened.
'My people are very unhappy in Egypt. They are slaves and are being treated very badly by the Egyptians.'
'I, I, I know', stuttered Moses – still rather taken aback to be talking to G-d in a bush!
'I have a special job for you, Moses.'
'Me?' said Moses, 'But I'm just a shepherd, and an old one at that.'
'I want you to go back to Egypt and tell the Pharaoh that he has got to let my people leave', said G-d.
'But Pharaoh won't listen to me,' replied Moses, '…I'm a hopeless speaker. I'll never persuade him.'
'I know that,' said G-d, 'but you can take your brother Aaron with you – he can talk! And I can give you some other ways of persuading the Pharaoh.'
'What sorts of ways?' asked Moses.
'Take the walking stick that's in your hand and throw it down on the floor.'
Moses did as he was told – and guess what happened! The stick changed into a wriggling snake!
'Now pick it up', ordered G-d. Moses wasn't very keen on snakes. He didn't fancy doing this at all! But then if G-d had the power to turn it into a snake in the first place – who knows what he could do! So Moses gritted his teeth, bent down and grabbed the wriggling snake. Straight away it turned back into a stick!
'Show that to the Pharaoh,' said G-d, 'that should persuade him. Now, Moses, put your shoes on and get going. My people need you.'
Moses knew it was useless to argue. If God thought he was the man for the job … well, he'd better just get on and do what he was told. He was glad he could take Aaron with him – at least he wouldn't face Pharaoh alone!
(Based on the Bible: Exodus chapters 3 and 4)

Activities for pupils

Lower primary activity: retelling the story using art and movement

- Engaging device: watch a candle flame flicker and dance. Focus on shapes, colours and feelings. Make a list of words about fire – how it feels, what it looks like, what fire can do. Talk about heat and danger. Is it safe to go near a fire? What happens when something catches fire? Why might a fire be a good symbol to show what G-d is like?
- Pupils could make burning bush collages using tissue and glitter paper. Display these with key words identified in the discussion around it.
- Tell the story of Moses from page 14 or a retelling based on a children's Bible version.
- In pairs pupils could role-play the burning bush scene: one pupil with orange, yellow and red streamers tied to wrist bands as the burning bush, the other, as Moses, in a long cloak from the dressing up box. Explore how Moses might feel when he sees the burning bush and hears G-d's voice. Talk about facial expressions and body language and explore how the burning bush might be portrayed.

- Retell the story whilst pupils perform the actions. Whenever G-d speaks, the 'flames' move more quickly. Record using a digital camera. Provide children with images and ask them to complete speech bubbles to record some of the things Moses and/or G-d said.
- Talk about how pupils might feel if they were asked to do a really important job (e.g. become the Head teacher or Prime Minister!). What would they need? Who would they choose to help them? What would be the first thing they would do in this job? Make the link to Moses being chosen to do a special job.

Upper primary activity: Moses – God's spokesman: using art and creative activities

- **The turning point.** Give pupils copies of the story on page 14. Ask them in pairs to put themselves in Moses' shoes and identify the turning point in the story. He was a humble shepherd – what made him agree to going back to Egypt and facing up to the Pharaoh? Pupils produce a picture or a piece of writing called 'The turning point'.
- **Character profile:** Pupils analyse the character of Moses from the information given in the story. What qualities does he have? What qualities will he need when he meets the Pharaoh. Imagine G-d had had to advertise for the right person for this special job. What would the advertisement say and show? Pupils could produce this advert. ICT graphics and wordart could be used.

See also...

These activities link with QCA RE scheme of work (2000) 1e 'How do Jewish people express their beliefs in practice?' sub-section: 'Why was Moses a leader?' www.topmarks.co.uk/judaism/moses/moses1.htm (Moses story for primary pupils) See pupils' artwork on the theme of the 'Turning Point' in the web gallery at www.pcfre.org.uk

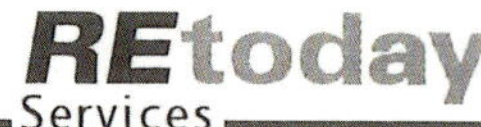

Moses and the Ten Commandments

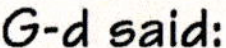

It was three months after the people of Israel had
escaped from slavery in Egypt and they were travelling
to freedom in the land G-d had promised to them.
Their leader was Moses and he wanted to make sure
that the people did not forget the greatness,
care and justice of G-d.
On their travels they reached Mount Sinai and
Moses knew that G-d would appear to the people.
Early in the morning the mountain was shrouded in thick cloud
and Moses led the people to the bottom to wait for G-d's message.
The mountain quaked and thick smoke appeared because G-d made his presence felt in fire.
G-d spoke to the people and gave them the rules (some say on tablets of stone)
on which Jews and Christians have based their lives ever since.

G-d said:

I am the Lord your G-d who brought you out of slavery in Egypt.
You shall have no other gods but me.
You shall not misuse the name of the Lord your G-d.
You shall remember and keep the Sabbath day holy.
Respect your father and mother.
You must not kill.
You must not commit adultery.
You must not steal.
You must not tell lies.
You must not be greedy or envious of your neighbour's goods.

This story can be found in the Jewish Torah (and in the Christian
Old Testament) in the Book of **Exodus chapters 19 and 20.**

Some key questions:

- Why do you think that there was
  cloud, smoke and fire when G-d
  appeared to the people? What
  does this 'detail' tell about how
  Jewish people think about G-d?
- Look carefully at the Ten
  Commandments. Can you explain
  how the first five are different
  from the last five?

Some key words:

G-d: many Jews do not write down the
name of G-d, believing that it breaks the
second commandment and might break the
third.
Moses: led the people out of slavery to
freedom.
Exodus: means 'going out'. The book of
Exodus is the second book of the Jewish
Torah and tells the story of how the Israelites
were freed from slavery in Egypt and
journeyed to the Promised Land.

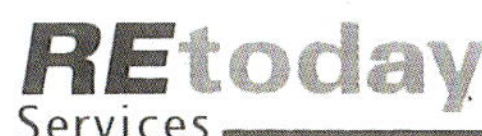

Activities for upper primary pupils: exploring a dilemma

Putting G-d's commandments into practice: a true story. *What should he do?*

'As I arrived in France for an important meeting I was looking forward to celebrating Shabbat (the Sabbath). Keeping Shabbat and all that it means is the central part of each week for us Jews. It shows both our obedience to, and our love for, the commandments of G-d.

'Then, out of the blue, I received a message from England that my elderly father had been taken into hospital and was asking for me. I did not know how serious his illness was. I found out about times for going home but I couldn't get back before sunset when Shabbat started, and travelling, or work of any kind, is forbidden on Shabbat for me as an Orthodox Jew. My mind was thrown into overdrive! What should I do? Should I compromise my belief in the importance of keeping Shabbat in order to get home quickly? What would my father want me to do? What would G-d want me to do?

'Keeping Shabbat is important (G-d commanded us to keep the seventh day holy as a way of honouring G-d) but G-d also laid down the commandment that we should honour our parents.
What should I do?'

Activity 1 (in pairs)

What would you do?

- Look at the Ten Commandments and decide which apply to this true story.
- What do you think the man should do? Why?
- What might you do if you were in a similar position. Why?

Activity 2 (in groups of 3 or 4)

- Make up a 'case study' based on a dilemma faced by someone trying to keep one (or more) of the Commandments.
  A simple one might focus on being in a position to steal something. A more complex one on a Jewish boy or girl being picked for the school football team and an important game coming up on Saturday morning.
- Role play the scenario, stopping where the decision has to be made. The class predicts what will happen, giving reasons. Have they guessed correctly? The group completes their presentation.

Fact file:

- Key questions (page 16) : the first five sayings are to do with G-d and people's relationship with G-d: the remaining five focus on how people should act towards others. The first four are to do with G-d but the rabbis teach that the relationship with parents is akin to the relationship with G-d because our parents created us and so to respect parents is to respect G-d.
- The Jewish festival of Shavuot remembers the people receiving the Ten Commandments. For further details see Page 13 of *Words of Wisdom,* (Developing Primary RE series, RE Today Services).

See also:

Some useful websites for use with pupils
www.holidays.net/shavuot/ten.htm–information about the festival of Shavuot;
www.amit.org.il/learning/english/lessons/shavuot/ –a site for Jewish children: some simple questions to try out;
www.topmarks.co.uk/judaism/commandments/ tencomms.htm basic outline of the ten commandments;
www.quran.org.uk/ieb_quran_10commandments. htm comparison between the commandments as laid out in Exodus and verses from the Qur'an.

Hindu stories about God

For the teacher

The following stories and activities aim to enable pupils to
- know the names and stories of some Hindu deities and be able to explain the characteristics of God they depict;
- ask questions about understandings of God and compare their own and other people's opinions of God.

Two stories about Brahman from Hindu scriptures

The Chandogya Upanishad (one of the holy books of Hinduism) includes the story of how a young boy named Svetaketu challenged his father to prove that God who is invisible actually exists.

Fact file: Hindu beliefs about God

- Hindus believe in one Supreme Being from whom everything comes. They call this supreme spirit Brahman.
- Hindus believe that each living thing–person, animal or plant embodies something of Brahman within them, but that humans have forgotten their real nature and fallen into a world of birth and death.
- Brahman has many aspects or faces and the many deities express these.
- Modern Hinduism places particular emphasis on the three gods Brahma (creator); Vishnu (preserver); Shiva (destroyer). Together these are known as the Trimurti.

The seed of the Banyan Tree

'Fetch me a fruit from the banyan tree and break it open', responded the father. 'Now take one of the seeds from inside the fruit and split it open.'

'What do you see?' asked the father. 'Nothing,' said the boy. 'There is nothing there.'
'But what would happen if you planted this seed?' asked the father.

'A great tree would grow', replied Svetaketu.
'Exactly', said the father. 'Inside that seed – not visible to the naked eye – is the most powerful source of life. In the same way, a great power pervades the entire universe. We may not be able to see it, but it exists.'

Seeing his son's interest the father went on further.

Salt in water

'What would happen if you mixed some salt into a bowl of water? Let's see, shall we?'
The father asked his son to mix the salt and water and leave it to dissolve. After a while he asked Svetaketu to taste the different parts and to separate the salt from the water.
'Every part of the water is salty', replied Svetaketu, 'and it's impossible to separate the salt from the water.'
'Well, in the same way as the salt is in every drop of water, Brahman (God) is in every bit of life. And just as salt cannot be separated from the water, all beings will finally merge with Brahman. Individuals may die but the Universal Spirit goes on and life itself therefore does not die.'

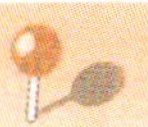

For the teacher

Use the activities described in the stories on page 18 to start older primary pupils thinking before telling the stories.

Looking at a seed

Show pupils a pomegranate *(banyan seeds are not easily available!)*.
Open the fruit and take out a seed. Ask pupils: 'What do you see?' Wait for responses.
Next ask pupils: 'What would happen if the seed was planted?' *(It grows into a tree 16 – 20 feet high.)*
Talk about how the seed is a source of life – but that we cannot see this with the naked eye.

Ask pupils: 'How might this story help some people think about God? What might it say about God?'

Salt and water

Show pupils a glass of water and some salt.
Ask: 'What would happen if we mixed salt into the water?'
Dissolve some salt in the water. Ask for volunteers to sip from different parts of the water and separate the salt from the water. How did they get on?
Draw parallels with how Hindus and others think about God. Just as we can't see the salt in the water, we can't see God. But for Hindus and other religions God is everywhere – not separate from other things. Hindus believe that Brahman is the source of all life, is everywhere, in all living things, has no shape, is not male or female but can take on many forms.

Activities for older primary pupils

Look at some pictures or statues of Hindu murtis (see:www.strath.ac.uk/Departments/ SocialStudies/RE/Database/Graphics/Images/ Hindu/Deities.html).
Explain to pupils that these **are visual aids** used to help Hindus focus on different characteristics of God, e.g. God as creator (Brahma); destroyer (Shiva); giver of wealth and prosperity (Lakshmi).

Experimenting with visual metaphor by creating their own images helps pupils to understand how visual images are used in Hinduism.

Activity – make your own visual personification
- Ask pupils individually to think what summer or winter might look like if portrayed as a person. Brainstorm the key features then think of things which symbolise these.
- What might a Lord of Learning or Goddess of Sport look like? What symbols and colours could be used?
- Explore the meaning of symbols used in the image of Durga (page 21). Design a visual personification for a 'Goddess of Goodness' for today (page 20). This activity encourages pupils to apply their learning about visual imagery in Hinduism and to use and interpret symbolism in a way similar to traditional Hindu iconography.

Activities for younger primary pupils:

Give children a sheet of paper with five circles on it. Ask them to draw their face when they are:

Ask: which one of these faces is you? Each face is you – but not the whole of you. Each is a little bit of you – what you can be like at different times – but not the whole of you.
Explain that this is how God is portrayed in Hinduism. Each representation of God gives insight into a part of God. God is believed to have many faces but there is one God.

See also:
Exploring the meaning of visual images in Hinduism:
Developing Primary RE:
Symbols of Faith page 19
(RE Today Services)

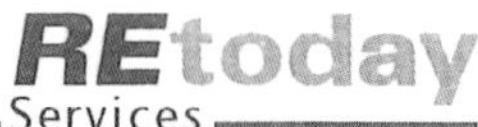

A story about the goddess Durga

Fact file: Durga

- Some Hindus like to think of God as their mother.
- Durga, also known as Parvati, is the wife of Lord Shiva and exists in various divine (both friendly and fearful) forms.
- Durga is a fierce and very powerful warrior goddess. She has eight or ten arms and great power and energy (Shakti). She rides a lion and holds many divine weapons. These are used to rid the world of evils and to foster growth and development.
- The story below is about good overcoming evil. Devotees of Durga are inspired by this story to actively stand up for what is right and good in the world today.

The story of Durga and the Buffalo Demon

Once long ago an evil demon called Mahishasura threatened to destroy the earth and all the gods. He was so powerful none of the gods could defeat him. They told Shiva about the terrible things the demon was doing. Shiva was angry. He opened his third eye and concentrated the energy coming out of it to form a woman. All the Gods present contributed the best of their powers to her and they called her Durga, the invincible one.

Riding a lion, Durga attacked Mahishasura, armed with the weapons from the gods – Shiva's trident, Vishnu's discus (wheel), Agni's dart, Surya's arrows and Indra's thunderbolt.

For a long time Durga battled against the demon army. When it was clear that she was winning the battle, the evil Mahishasura flew into a terrible rage. He became a ferocious male buffalo and thundered towards Durga, lashing out with his horns, his hooves and his tail, and killing many of her followers. The earth shook and the waters foamed.

A great battle followed. Durga managed to lasso him, but as she did so he turned into a lion and escaped. Durga chased after him, cutting off his head. But again he changed – this time into a man. Next Durga shot the man with arrows – but again he changed, this time into an elephant. She battled on, cutting off the elephant's trunk. But the evil Mahishasura now turned back again into a buffalo. Durga was not to be defeated. Using all her strength she pinned him down with a foot on his neck, and plunged Shiva's trident into him. She cut off his terrible head with her sword. At last the demon Mahishasura was dead. The gods rejoiced. 'Durga, we praise you!' they cried. 'You who destroy evil and uphold goodness.'

Activities for older primary pupils

- Pupils could read or listen to the story of Durga and the Buffalo demon. Look at an image of Durga (such as that on the website suggested on page 21).
- Ask pupils in pairs to consider: What qualities does Durga have? What does 'evil' mean? Are there evil things in the world today? What qualities do we need to stand up for what is right and good?
- Pupils complete the activity sheet on page 21.
- Pupils could design their own 'superhero' figure based on Durga. As with Durga, you should give this figure gifts and powers to overcome bad things in the world today and be able to explain their thinking.

Durga and the Buffalo Demon

_________________ the evil _______________

Evil: we think this means   _______________________________________

____

Some evil things today are: ____

____

In order to stand up against evil or bad things today we need to ____________________

____

Missing words:

arrow	sword	demon	mace	discus (disc)	thunderbolt
Mahishasura	conch shell	shield	dart	lion	

In this unit of work you will be doing well if you can…
- explain the story behind this Durga image and say what it means for Hindus
- use your learning to design your own superhero 'Goddess of goodness', explaining the symbols used.

See also…

For an animated version of this picture see: www.hindu kids.org/pray/god_goddesses /durga/index.

The story of Prahlad

For the teacher

- This story reminds Hindus of the rewards of loyalty and devotion to God and how faith can overcome evil.
- It is often told at the Hindu festival of Holi, when bonfires are lit and roasting grains (called Holuk), pop corn, coconut and chick peas are thrown on by Hindu families.

Once upon a time there was an evil king called Hiranyakashipu (which means 'dressed in gold') who demanded that everyone should worship him as a god. He thought of himself as the 'Lord of the universe', but his son Prahlad would only worship the great God Vishnu. The king tried to force his son to bow down to him, but Prahlad refused.

The king ordered his army to kill his son, but Prahlad called on the great god Vishnu and the soldiers lost their strength. Then the king had him thrown into a pit of poisonous snakes, but again Prahlad called on Vishnu and survived. The king tried many ways to kill the boy, but every time Prahlad called on Vishnu and was saved.

In the end, the evil king called on his sister Holika to carry Prahlad into the flames of a bonfire. She had been promised that she had a gift from the gods that would save her from being burnt. The evil Holika cackled with laughter as the flames began to rise around her and Prahlad. But again he called 'Vishnu, Vishnu!' and the power of the Vishnu was so great that Prahlad was protected while Holika was burned.

Hours later, the king came to watch the dying fire. No courtier dared to warn him what he would find. There on the mound of ash sat Prahlad. 'God saved me', said Prahlad, simply. 'I'm sick of your God,' said the King. 'Where is this God, then? See if he'll save you from me.' The king drew his sword.
'God is everywhere,' said Prahlad. 'He is in the fire, in water, in the wind and the grass, even in that stone column behind you.'

With that the column broke in two. Out came God but his shape was strange. The upper part of his body was that of a lion, the lower that of a man. He was neither man nor animal. He lifted the king, carried him to the palace door and placed him on his lap. Then he killed him with a single swipe of his great claws. Vishnu made Prahlad the king and he ruled wisely and well ever after.

See also:

Websites: A pupil-friendly website on Hinduism with links to other appropriate sites:
www.ict.mic.ul.ie/websites/2002/Aisling_OMahony/Homepage.htm

Things to note:

The stories and activities in this Hinduism section fit well with the following QCA schemes of work (2000):

- 3A What do signs and symbols mean in religion?
- 3B How and why do Hindus celebrate Divali?
- 4A How and why do Hindus worship at home and in the mandir?

For the teacher

Good use of the stories will develop pupils' understanding by getting them to work with the story, rather than simply retell it. Two activities for doing this are given below.

• Use the story of Prahlad with the target board diagram and ask pupils to work (in pairs) to show their understanding of what matters most to Prahlad. One statement only goes in the centre, no more than two in each of the other circles. This activity requires pupils to reflect, evaluate and justify their ideas. It provides opportunities for pupils to show achievement at level three of the QCA scale of expectations.

• By asking children to reflect on what some Hindu children have said about God and matching these to the experiences of Prahlad in the story, pupils should be able to identify and talk about some key Hindu beliefs about God.

Activities for pupils

1. What mattered most to Prahlad

Obeying his father
Becoming king
Living in a palace
Trusting Vishnu
Being admired by other people
Believing that God was in everything and everyone
Living dangerously
Standing up for what was right
Praying
Being good

2. What might a young Hindu learn from this story?

• Below are a series of statements Hindu children your age have said about God.
• In pairs talk about how these match up to the beliefs and experiences of Prahlad in the story.
• Make a list of adjectives to describe God that fit with both the story and the children's ideas.
• Write your own statement about what you think or believe about God. Add your own statement to the website for others to read:
www.pcfre.org.uk/db/primary.php

What some young Hindus say about God:

God is around to protect us

Hindu girl aged 9

I believe that you should obey God and never disobey him. You should always try and follow God

Hindu boy aged 8

I believe in God because he or she gives us things we need

Hindu boy aged 9

I think God warns you and helps you. God is all around you and he will always be there for you

Hindu girl aged 10

I think God is a loving person no matter the bad things he makes happen because he does it for their own good. I also think God is more powerful than all of us

Hindu girl aged 10

I believe that wherever you go he is always there looking after us

Hindu girl aged 11

Muslim stories about Allah from the life of Prophet Muhammad (pbuh)

For the teacher

The revelation of the Qur'an to Prophet Muhammad (pbuh) (Lailat ul Qadr or Night of Power) and his Night Journey (Isra) and Ascension (Miraj) are powerful stories which provide insights into some key aspects of Muslim belief:

- Why is Prophet Muhammad (pbuh) important?
- How and why does Allah communicate with people?
- How are beliefs shown through what people do?
- Why is the Qur'an important?
- What is the role of angels?

The activities suggested here provide ways into thinking about such aspects of belief suitable for older primary pupils.

They complement the QCA non-statutory schemes for RE (2000) which focus on Islam (units 5A, 5B and 6D).

See also:

Websites
- BBC Religion: This site provides a clear overview of the main aspects of Islam. www.bbc.co.uk/religion/religions/islam
- Islam4schools: A clear Q & A style introduction to Prophet Muhammad. www.islam4schools.com/prophet-mohd.htm
- Stories of the Prophets :A Shi'a Muslim site which provides a collection of stories of the main prophets of Islam for children. al-islam.org/gallery/kids/Books/stories/index.htm

Books:
- Marvellous stories from the Life of Muhammad, Mardijah Aldrich Tarantino (The Islamic Foundation, 2003, ISBN 0 86037 103 4) www.islamic-foundation.org.uk
- Islam: A Pictorial Guide (RE Today, 3rd Edition, 2003, ISBN 1-904024-35-1) www.retoday.org.uk

Fact file: Muslim beliefs about God: Allah

Muslims believe that there is one God, **Allah**, and he has revealed his will through the **Qur'an** – the Holy Book which was revealed to **Prophet Muhammad (pbuh)**.

The Shahadah is the declaration of faith for Muslims. It affirms that there is no God but Allah and Muhammad (pbuh) is the messenger of Allah. The Shahadah is the first pillar of Islam.

Allah is One, and the only one deserving of praise and worship. Allah is described by **ninety-nine beautiful names** which each tell something different about the nature of Allah. There are only ninety-nine names because only Allah knows everything. Muslims often use the phrase **'Bismillah'**, which means 'in the name of Allah'.

Expectations

It is important to be clear about what you want pupils to know, understand and be able to do by the end of the teaching activity.

Below you will see three 'I can' statements which describe such outcomes in a pupil-friendly way. These are based on the QCA's expectations for most-nine-year olds in RE, matched to the content of the teaching unit.

I can...

- respond sensitively to stories about people from the Muslim religion, noticing what matters to them (level 2)
- ask some questions and suggest some answers about what I could learn from Muslim stories and beliefs (level 3)
- ask some questions and suggest some answers from Islam about life's mysteries, giving my own view on the questions (level 4).

The story of the Night of Power – the Qur'an is revealed to Muhammad (pbuh)

The city of Makkah was hot and sticky, and crowded with many visitors. Muhammad (pbuh) had just returned from a long trip, and wanted to get away from the busy and noisy city to somewhere quiet and peaceful where he could be alone to talk to God.

He told his wife, Khadijah, that he was going to the cave called Hira in the nearby mountains. It was a cave he often went to when he wanted to think and pray.

The cave was quiet and cool. At last he had some time to pray and to be alone to think. Suddenly he had a strange feeling. He felt as though he wasn't alone, that someone else was there! He slowly turned around, and in the corner near the entrance to the cave he could see a light. He looked more closely, squinting his eyes to get a better view. Then he realised it wasn't a light at all – it was an angel! The angel, who was called Jibril, held out a scroll of paper which had words written on it. 'Read this, Muhammad', the angel said. 'But I can't read', replied Muhammad. Once again the angel told him to read the words on the scroll, and once again, Muhammad told the angel that he could not read. A third time the angel told him to read the scroll, in the name of the Lord who created the world.

This time Muhammad found that he could read the words on the scroll, and as he read them he felt as though the words were being written on his heart. Muhammad repeated the words, and then he knew that he would never forget them.

Muhammad left the cave and returned to the city of Makkah to tell his wife, Khadijah, all about what had happened to him in the cave. She knew immediately just how important these words were. She realised the words were from God.

In the following months and years Muhammad received many more words from God, and he told them to many people who also believed they were from God. Some people in Makkah believed what he said was true, and others did not like what he was saying.

Years later, Muhammad died. Then the people who believed what Muhammad had said to be true wrote down all the words that Muhammad had been told by the angel Jibril, so that the words would never be forgotten. The book they were written in is called the Qur'an. The word Qur'an means 'that which is read or recited.'

Today the events of this remarkable night are celebrated at the festival of Lailat al Qadr on the 27th day of the month of Ramadan.

For the teacher
Fortune line activity

The following activity uses the thinking skills strategy known as a fortune line or feelings graph. This strategy enables pupils to engage deeply with a chosen piece of text. It challenges them to interpret information by organising it within a familiar visual structure – a graph.

The Night of Power: How did Muhammad (pbuh) feel?

Getting started

- Ask pupils to imagine that their best friend tells them something amazing about themselves (which could possibly be true) e.g. that they have met a famous person. Pupils **suggest** questions they could ask to try and find out whether the person was telling the truth. **Record** suggestions on the board, and then ask pupils to sort the questions into good and weak.

Exploring the story

- Read the story on page 25 with the pupils.
- **Provide** pupils in pairs with a copy of a grid (see example below) and a set of the nine cards given below. Ask them to:
  - **sequence** the cards to re-tell the story they have just heard;
  - **talk about** each card in turn and **place** it on the graph according to the point in the story it occurred (x axis) and how they think Muhammad (pbuh) felt (y axis);
  - **feed back** to the whole class their decisions, reasons and any questions;
  - **annotate** their grid with anything they want to record, e.g. unresolved questions.
- Pupils **consider** the questions they suggested would help find out if someone was telling the truth – and **decide** which of these Khadijah might have asked. They then write the diary entry Khadijah might have written to a friend about the remarkable events, reflecting her questions and feelings.

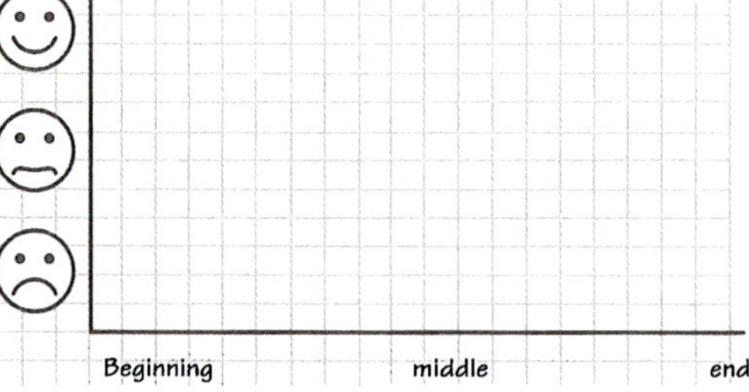

Muhammad returns to Makkah from a long trip. He is hot and very tired.	Muhammad goes to a cave at Hira, to pray to God and enjoy the peacefulness.	Suddenly Muhammad feels he is not alone. The Angel Jibril is beside him.
Jibril insists that Muhammad reads from a scroll, even when he protests that he cannot read.	Eventually Muhammad reads the words! He repeats them to help him remember them.	Muhammad goes home and tells Khadijah, his wife, all that has happened.
Muhammad wonders what he will do if Khadijah doesn't believe him.	Eventually Khadijah says that she believes that the words are from God.	Muhammad tells many other people what happened. Not everyone believes him.

The story of Muhammad's (pbuh) night journey and ascension

Muhammad (pbuh) was sound asleep when a voice called him so insistently that he woke up. There before him stood the angel Jibril in full splendour. Jibril beckoned for him to follow and when they reached the doorway Muhammad saw a most marvellous beast. This was Burraq – a dazzling white mare with a human face, wings like an eagle, hooves which reached as far as the eye could see, and the ability to travel faster than light. Jibril told Muhammad to mount the creature, and together they flew off into the night sky, leaving Makkah far behind.

All along the journey they saw many strange and terrible sights. Some were designed to tempt the Prophet and lead him from the true path, others were examples of the terrible punishments which people bring upon themselves as a result of the things they do on earth.

At last they landed at the gates of the temple in Jerusalem. As they entered they saw Jesus and Moses and many other prophets. After spending some time in prayer they came out, and there was another wondrous thing. Reaching all the way up into the heavens was a Ladder of Light. Jibril told Muhammad to mount the Ladder, and he did so, as quickly and easily as if it had been made of air.

Moses then led Muhammad through each of seven heavens. They met many prophets from the past including Adam, Noah, Aaron, Moses, John the Baptist and Jesus. They also saw many great and powerful angels who existed to offer praise and worship to God, to punish those who disobeyed him and to encourage and reward those who were faithful.

Finally, Muhammad was taken into the Heavenly Abode, into the presence of God. There was a sweet fragrance all around, and Muhammad felt the touch of an invisible hand on his shoulder and chest which produced a feeling of unspeakable happiness. Here he was given the laws which govern Islam.

On his descent from the Heavenly Abode the Prophet met again with Moses. 'How many prayers a day are prescribed for your religion?' asked Moses. 'Fifty prayers a day,' responded the Prophet. Moses was troubled. 'Muhammad, how do you imagine that your people will pray fifty times a day? Believe me, people are quite incapable of carrying out such an instruction. Go back – and ask for a smaller number.'

So Muhammad returned and asked for fewer prayers. On his way back down, he met with Moses again, who asked him, 'How many prayers are prescribed to you now?' 'Forty,' replied Muhammad. 'Forty!!! Impossible! Go back and ask for fewer.'

And so the situation continued. Even when Muhammad reported that just five prayers a day were required, Moses said, 'That is still too much. Imagine an ordinary man praying five times a day! Return again!' 'No,' answered Muhammad. 'I have returned too many times and I am ashamed.' He then said goodbye to Moses and began his descent.

Down they went, by the Ladder of Light, back to the temple in Jerusalem. When they reached it they found Burraq and flew back to the house where Jibril had found Muhammad sleeping.

Today the events of this remarkable night are celebrated at the festival of Lailat al Miraj on the 27th day of the month of Rajab.

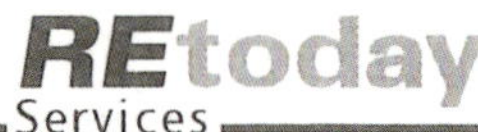

Activities for upper primary pupils
Muhammad's night journey – a turning point

For the teacher

The events of this story represent something of a turning point for Muhammad (pbuh). At the time, he was at a very low ebb. His much-loved wife, Khadijah, had recently died, as had the uncle (Abu Talib) who had brought him up. He was also having a hard time convincing some people of the truth of what he was saying.

The experience of the Night Journey restored Muhammad's (pbuh) faith. He felt convinced of his role as a prophet – that he was chosen by God. Explaining this background will help pupils set the story in context and help them decide on its essential meaning.

Feelings box

A feelings box is a simple strategy to help pupils analyse, reflect on and express a range of feelings. Ideally it consists of a 3D box (e.g. a shoe box) containing laminated cards with words describing a full spectrum of human emotions. Put a range of carefully selected words inside the box to complement the story. Pupils choose a character from the story. They can either pass the box round, with each pupil picking out a word which describes how that character might have felt and explaining their thinking, or highlight their chosen word on the whiteboard.

Activities for pupils

1. **Prepare a feelings box,** using the feelings included on this page as a starting point.

2. **Read the story** of Muhammad's (pbuh) Night Journey and Ascension (page 27) and then:
   - use the feelings box to explore how he might have felt before and after the event.
   - pupils work in pairs to identify the point of view from which the story is told and how this affects their response to it. They feed back ideas to the class.
   - pupils work in pairs to re-tell the story from the point of view of one of the following: someone who doesn't believe that Muhammad (pbuh) is telling the truth; Prophet Muhammad (pbuh); Angel Jibril. It is helpful if pupils have the text available electronically on a whiteboard to encourage them to focus on meaning and interpretation.

3. **Talk, write and do:**
   Pick out the part of the story which tells the most about Allah
   - What do you think Allah is like?
   - What words might a Muslim use to describe him?

Look up the 99 beautiful names of Allah on a website and pick out those which match best with the story. Try:
www.dawateislami.net/general/devotions/99names/

www.islam4schools.com/Allah.htm

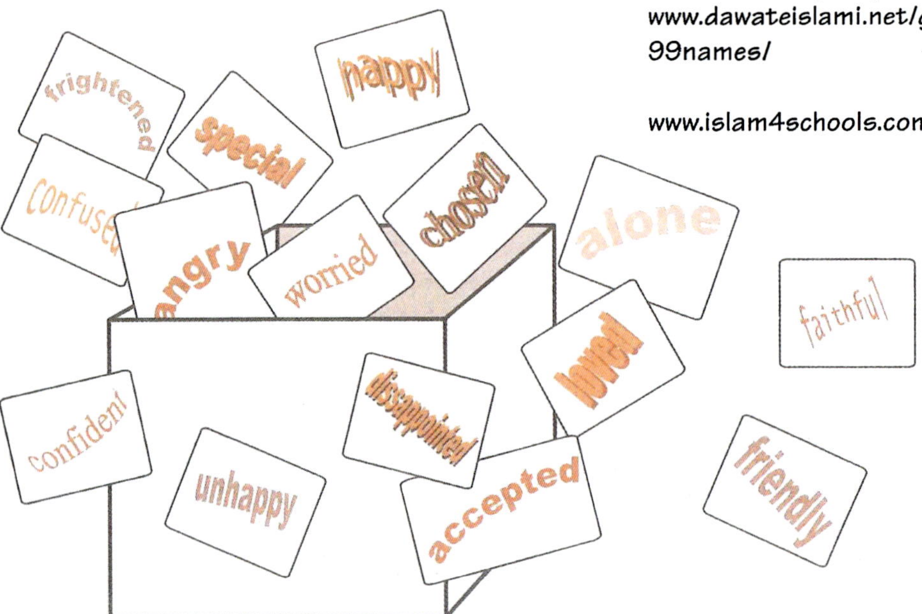

Two Sikh stories about God

For the teacher

When exploring the stories on these pages you may find the following questions useful as a focus:

- What is the key idea of each story?
  For Sikhs? For me?
- What do these stories teach about God?
  Where is God?
  What is God like?
  What do I think about God?
- What do I agree/disagree with in the stories?

Expectations

If pupils are to do well, it is important to be clear about what you want pupils to know, understand and be able to do by the end of any teaching activity. Share this with pupils so that they know what is expected of them. Below you will see some 'I can' statements which describe such outcomes in a pupil-friendly way. These are based on the QCA expectations matched to the content of this teaching unit.

- I can describe what happens in two Sikh stories, say what they mean and make some links between them (AT1) and I can compare those meanings with what I think. (AT2) (Level 3)

- I can understand and use correctly the special words connected to the stories (e.g. sakhis, ritual, Guru, etc.) (AT1) and suggest why Guru Nanak said the things he did in the stories and give my own thoughtful comments about these. (AT2) (Level 4)

- I can interpret the meaning of the stories and compare and contrast these with a story from another religion (AT1) giving thoughtful reasons why I agree or disagree with any of the ideas within the stories. (Level 5)

Fact file: Sikh beliefs about God One God – eternal truth

- Sikhs believe in one God.
- Guru Nanak, the first Sikh Guru, taught that God is present everywhere and within the human heart and is not found in any particular image or place.
- God is described in the Mool Mantar, the opening verses of the Guru Granth Sahib (the Sikh holy book). God is one, truth, the creator, fearless, without hatred, beyond time, not incarnated, self-existent and made known to humans by the Guru (teacher).
- Ik Onkar – there is only one God – the first phrase of the Mool Mantar, is often used as a symbol in Sikhism.

See also:
For fuller versions of these and other stories suitable for primary pupils see:
www.ikonkar.com/sikhism/Sakis/Sakis.htm 16 sakhis (stories of the gurus)
www.sln.org.uk/storyboard/l6.htm 5 Sikh stories

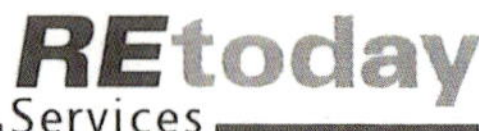

Guru Nanak asks an important question – Where is God?

On one of his many travels Guru Nanak visited the Muslim holy city of Makkah. He was very tired from his journey and fell asleep in the courtyard. Whilst he was asleep his feet turned towards the Kabbah (cube-shaped structure in the centre of the grand mosque, believed by Muslims to be the first house built for the worship of the One True God). This upset some of those present since to point your feet towards this holy place was an insult. Some people woke the Guru up and said to him, 'You are supposed to be a holy man, and yet you do something so disrespectful to God. How could you?'

The Guru did not want to upset anyone and certainly did not want to be disrespectful towards God. He replied to their criticism. 'I'm sorry – could you point my feet in a direction where they will not be pointing at God?'

What do you think he meant by this?
How do you think the people reacted to this?

Guru Nanak asks an important question – Is ritual useless?

Guru Nanak visited Hardwar, a town by the river Ganges in India. He watched people throw handfuls of water from the river towards the sun in the east. They thought that by this ritual they could offer water to their dead relatives in the next world.

The Guru went into the river and started throwing water towards the west. Everyone looked at him and laughed. 'Why are you throwing the water the wrong way?' they asked. Guru Nanak answered, 'I am watering my withering crops in the Punjab.' 'Are you crazy?' they replied. 'How can your water reach hundreds of miles away from here?'

'The very same way as yours reaches your ancestors in the other world', was his swift reply.

What do you think this made the people think about?
How do you think the people reacted?

Two Sikh stories about God

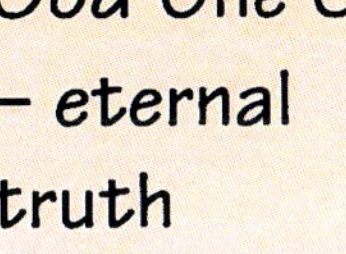

For the teacher

When exploring the stories on these pages you may find the following questions useful as a focus:

- What is the key idea of each story?
  For Sikhs? For me?
- What do these stories teach about God?
  Where is God?
  What is God like?
  What do I think about God?
- What do I agree/disagree with in the stories?

Expectations

If pupils are to do well, it is important to be clear about what you want pupils to know, understand and be able to do by the end of any teaching activity. Share this with pupils so that they know what is expected of them. Below you will see some 'I can' statements which describe such outcomes in a pupil-friendly way. These are based on the QCA expectations matched to the content of this teaching unit.

- I can describe what happens in two Sikh stories, say what they mean and make some links between them (AT1) and I can compare those meanings with what I think. (AT2) (Level 3)

- I can understand and use correctly the special words connected to the stories (e.g. sakhis, ritual, Guru, etc.) (AT1) and suggest why Guru Nanak said the things he did in the stories and give my own thoughtful comments about these. (AT2) (Level 4)

- I can interpret the meaning of the stories and compare and contrast these with a story from another religion (AT1) giving thoughtful reasons why I agree or disagree with any of the ideas within the stories. (Level 5)

Fact file: Sikh beliefs about God One God – eternal truth

- Sikhs believe in one God.
- Guru Nanak, the first Sikh Guru, taught that God is present everywhere and within the human heart and is not found in any particular image or place.
- God is described in the Mool Mantar, the opening verses of the Guru Granth Sahib (the Sikh holy book). God is one, truth, the creator, fearless, without hatred, beyond time, not incarnated, self-existent and made known to humans by the Guru (teacher).
- Ik Onkar – there is only one God – the first phrase of the Mool Mantar, is often used as a symbol in Sikhism.

See also:
For fuller versions of these and other stories suitable for primary pupils see:
www.ikonkar.com/sikhism/Sakis/Sakis.htm 16 sakhis (stories of the gurus)
www.sln.org.uk/storyboard/l6.htm
5 Sikh stories

Guru Nanak asks an important question – Where is God?

On one of his many travels Guru Nanak visited the Muslim holy city of Makkah. He was very tired from his journey and fell asleep in the courtyard. Whilst he was asleep his feet turned towards the Kabbah (cube-shaped structure in the centre of the grand mosque, believed by Muslims to be the first house built for the worship of the One True God). This upset some of those present since to point your feet towards this holy place was an insult. Some people woke the Guru up and said to him, 'You are supposed to be a holy man, and yet you do something so disrespectful to God. How could you?'

The Guru did not want to upset anyone and certainly did not want to be disrespectful towards God. He replied to their criticism. 'I'm sorry – could you point my feet in a direction where they will not be pointing at God?'

What do you think he meant by this?
How do you think the people reacted to this?

Guru Nanak asks an important question - Is ritual useless?

Guru Nanak visited Hardwar, a town by the river Ganges in India. He watched people throw handfuls of water from the river towards the sun in the east. They thought that by this ritual they could offer water to their dead relatives in the next world.

The Guru went into the river and started throwing water towards the west. Everyone looked at him and laughed. 'Why are you throwing the water the wrong way?' they asked. Guru Nanak answered, 'I am watering my withering crops in the Punjab.' 'Are you crazy?' they replied. 'How can your water reach hundreds of miles away from here?'

'The very same way as yours reaches your ancestors in the other world', was his swift reply.

What do you think this made the people think about?
How do you think the people reacted?

Activities for pupils

Activity 1
Transporting Guru Nanak

Imagine Guru Nanak visited us instead of visiting Makkah or Hardwar. How would he get across the same message from each story in Manchester or Hemel Hempstead?

In small groups: devise a short drama or role play.

Activity 2
Diary entry

Imagine you are one of the people who heard what Guru Nanak said (in either Makkah or Hardwar). You have been thinking about it and puzzling over it all day. You are in the habit of keeping a daily diary.

Individually: write your diary entry for this day.

Activity 3
Making Music

Imagine that each story is going to be a scene in a film about the life of Guru Nanak. You have the script but you have to provide the musical backing.

In pairs or threes: make up the music using the instruments provided by your teacher.

Activity 4
Zoom lens or target board

For the teacher

- Provide enough target boards for pupils to work in pairs – A3 paper/card on which are drawn four concentric circles, like a 'bulls-eye' on a dartboard – see illustration.

- Pupils discuss the statements in the light of the stories and place each on the target board where they think Guru Nanak would place it. Record answers. Repeat activity placing the statements to express their own ideas. Record answers.

- Two pairs join to compare results. Where do they agree/disagree with 'Guru Nanak' and with each other?

- Feed back to class. If available, use interactive whiteboard technology to record similarities and differences in graph form.

Being respectful to God	Being respectful to other people
Doing the right thing	Taking part in religious services
Not upsetting people	Challenging other people to do the right thing
Talking to others about God	Making fun of other people
Making other agree with him/me	Not getting laughed at
Believing in life after death	Saying prayers and worshipping God

Talking to children about God: ten tips for teachers

Religious education is energised and made inspiring when teachers boldly enter the tentative and unknown territory of God-talk with young children. But many teachers don't like saying 'I don't know' to children, and don't feel confident in dealing with the plurality of beliefs – Allah, Brahman, Trinity and the True Name of the Almighty seems territory fit for professors, not 7-year-olds. So these ten tips might make it easier for teachers to enable good, intriguing, rigorous God-talk with their pupils.

1. Admit you don't know.
All knowledge is bounded by mystery, and when we do truth-seeking in uncertain fields, it is wise to admit that we are ignorant. Sharing this with the pupils shows them the God-questions are mysterious for adults too.

2. Ask great questions.
Teachers who plan their questions find out how useful it is. Ask: 'This religion says God is full of love – any thoughts on that?' And wait 5 seconds for the hands to creep up.

3. Delight in diversity.
Good RE and thoughtful children know that there are many answers to God-questions. Seek them out by asking, even the young ones, 'Has anyone got a different idea?'

4. Use stories from sacred text.
Religions teach about God through story. It's often a better route than through creeds, and not just for children! Tell the stories, never edit God out, and ask the children to think. Use the literacy strategy's many techniques to guide the conversation skilfully.

5. Answer a question with a question.
'But, miss, how can God answer all the prayers?' 'Well, Danny, do you think angels are like secretaries?' This old teacher habit always takes us further, but keep open-ended development of views in the frame.

6. Give access to the specifics within the faiths.
Muslims believe Allah is beyond representation. Christians think God was born in Jesus. Without ever closing the distance between the faiths, they still have a lot in common. Aim to use authentic ideas and resources from within each faith.

7. Aim for encounter.
RE's highest aspirations are served when views rub up against each other, and pupils learn to disagree respectfully. Set up encounters with visits and visitors to talk about God together, not just to label the diagram of the font!

8. Be happy without conclusions.
The quest for God is a lifelong personal quest for some, and a big-scale human enterprise lasting thousands of years. Treasuring the questions is one way of closing in on some answers. Good RE is happy to pursue the conversation rigorously, not to put a full stop at the end.

9. Welcome language-playfulness.
One aim of RE might be to enable pupils to achieve 'playful ease' in their God-talk. Asking about metaphors – like the paracetamol at the bottom of the page – is a great example of this playfulness.

10. Never imagine you've even nearly finished.
Atheists and theologians alike from many traditions continue to refine their God-talk for life. Make this a topic for lifelong learning for any pupil.

See also
The Spirit of the Child (Hay and Nye, Fount, 1998)
Faith in the future An anthology of children's comments (RE Today Services ISBN1-85100-136-0).

'God is like a huge paracetemol dissolved in water. All the dissolved bits are spread around this earth and also everywhere else. Each bit of paracetemol is able to see, hear and take care of us. It can also communicate with us. At the end of this world, all the bits will come together and form a huge (but still approachable) person – whose image we were made in.'
Clare (a 14-year-old Christian pupil).